ABOUT THE BOOK

Many people think hang gliders are weird lashed-together contraptions made out of bamboo and plastic, and the pilots a curious breed of thrill-seeking death wishers. But although it *is* a high-risk sport, the pioneering days of hang gliding have long since passed. Modern hang gliders are factory-made and tested, and their pilots range from twelve-year-old boys to eighty-year-old grandmothers.

Always emphasizing the need to establish and maintain proper safety precautions, author Ross R. Olney describes here the joys of hang gliding and advises beginners on the procedures to follow to ensure a safe and happy flight the first time and *every* time.

HANG GLIDING

BY ROSS R. OLNEY

G. P. PUTNAM'S SONS / NEW YORK

PHOTO CREDITS

Courtesy of:
Bill Bennett, pp. 32, 48, 91, 109
Chan Bush, pp. 13, 17, 21, 44, 61
Free Flight Systems, pp. 35, 93
Rich Grigsby, pp. 54, 81
Ross D. Olney, pp. 36, 53, 56, 59, 60
Ross R. Olney, pp. 15, 16, 103, 104, 107

Copyright © 1976 by Ross R. Olney
All rights reserved. Published simultaneously in
Canada by Longman Canada Limited, Toronto.
SBN: GB–399–61027–8
SBN: TR–399–20537–3
PRINTED IN THE UNITED STATES OF AMERICA
12 up

Library of Congress Cataloging in Publication Data

Odney, Ross Robert, 1929–
Hang Gliding

Includes index
    SUMMARY: Describes the equipment and techniques
of hang gliding.
1.   Hang gliding—Juvenile literature.   [1.   Hang
gliding.   2.   Hang gliders]   I.   Title.
GV764.045   797.5'5   76–16193

CONTENTS

The author would like to thank the following for photos, advice, and technical information:

Mike Addison, Southern California School of Hang Gliding
Gerald Albiston, Free-Flight Systems
George Barker, pilot
Bill Bennett, Delta Wing Kites and Gliders
Pete and Hall Brock, Ultralite Products
Dennis Burton, altitude record holder
Chan Bush, photographer
Richard Grigsby, United States Hang Gliding Association and
    Southern California School of Hang Gliding
Ross D. Olney, pilot, photographer and darkroom technician

and especially Gary Vallé of Sunbird Gliders, who was generous with advice and technical information and who firmly believes that hang gliding is not only here to stay, but is the greatest sport of all.

HANG GLIDING

When they learn that you are flying, and they say, as they surely will, "If God had meant you to fly, he would have given you wings," say to them, "If God had meant you *not* to fly, he would have given you roots." —IRV CULVER, aerodynamicist

1/FLYING THE HANG GLIDER

Flying a hang glider for the very first time is twice as thrilling and demands twice the courage as flying it for the second, or the fiftieth, time. You stand there on some windy hill, and *no one* can tell you it's only a bunny hill. But you *have* been thoroughly trained, so you know exactly what to expect. Finally, everyone else has flown, and they turn to you: "Well, are you going or not?"

The chips are down. You don the harness, put on the helmet, and select a glider. "What am I doing here?" you ask yourself. Over you, the glider is no longer graceful and beautiful, but heavy, and pulling you all the wrong ways in the wind. Somehow it seemed much easier and more sensible in the simulator at the hang gliding school.

The wind buffets the kite, tightening the sling in unexpected places. Activity on the beach below seems to stop. Everyone is watching.

"Ready?" shouts the instructor from the rear, his hand solidly on the keel. He is prepared to run with you all the way to the edge.

Your voice caught in your throat, you swallow. "Ready," you say, softer than usual. Maybe he won't hear.

He hears. "Run," he orders. "Run! Run! Run!"

You both run forward toward the edge with the sound of cheers in the background. The wind whips at the glider and at your face. You can feel the instructor pushing against the glider to increase speed. Time is suspended. *What* are you doing? The dropoff approaches. Stop!

It is a *Grand Canyon!*

You've made a terrible mistake. Just at the moment you realize this and decide to dig in and stop before it's too late, you feel the sail fill and the harness lift you by the backside.

You are *flying!*

"Push out . . . push out!" shouts the instructor from behind. He is still with you, his hand on the keel. You push out on the control bar, and the glider lifts away from the ground. Remembering, you pull it back an instant before you hear him say, "Pull back!"

In a series of short stalls, for a flight of five seconds or so, you go downward. The landing is not gentle, but it's not a crash either. You are exhilarated. Experienced hang gliders say no matter how many flights you make or how many contests you enter, you will always remember that first flight, short though it may be.

What are you doing here? Now you know as you start back up the slope for flight number two.

The time has long since passed when a hang glider was thought to be a lashed-together contraption about as safe as a dime-store kite and a hang glider pilot a questionably intelligent, devil-may-care character who thrilled in risking his life. Like sailplaning, motorcycling, surfing, skin diving, and many other activities for the somewhat more daring, hang gliding has grown out of the zany phase to become an accepted sport.

"More daring" is a carefully chosen description, for hang gliding will never be for the fainthearted. No matter how far the sport has gone, no matter how certain everyone is that the glider is safe, it takes courage to run as fast as you can over the edge of a cliff with nothing more than a forty-pound framework of aluminum and Dacron between you and eternity. Even some sky divers balk at the cliff edge—and *they* throw themselves from the doors of airplanes for fun.

There was a time when a hang glider was whatever its pilot wanted to call it. Some pioneers went to the cliffs with weird contraptions made of bamboo and sandwich bags.

A modern hang glider is carefully designed and fully tested. Gary Vallé, president of Sunbird Gliders, or one of his pilots tests every glider manufactured by his company. This procedure is also followed by Pete Brock, who gained fame as the designer of the Shelby Cobra and other fine automobiles before he turned full time to hang gliding, and by Gerald Albiston, of Free Flight Systems, as well as by most other glider manufacturers.

There are two basic types of hang gliders in general manufacture and use today: the flexible delta-shaped Rogallo-wing glider, and the fixed-wing airfoil-shaped glider similar to

Gary Vallé testing a hang glider at Sylmar in California.

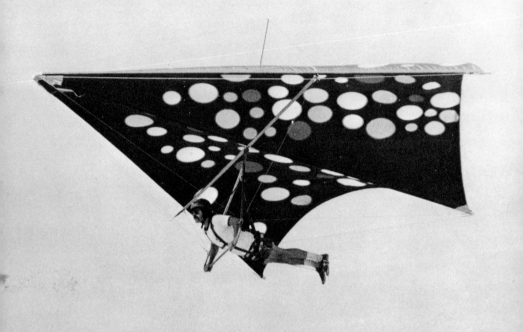

The two basic types of hang gliders are the Rogallo wing type . . .

. . . and the fixed wing type.

the one the Wright brothers used at Kitty Hawk. Yes, the Wright brothers were pioneer hang gliders before they decided to attach a motor to their flying machine.

Some hang gliders even have controls and simple instrumentation, but there is one thing that qualifies all these aircraft as hang gliders (and thus, at least for now, frees them from Federal Aviation Administration regulations): All of them are *pilot launched.*

There are manufacturers who build "sky kites" and other towed devices, but these are not to be confused with true hang gliders. A hang glider is launched by its pilot from a hill or a cliff or some other high place or is dropped from another aircraft, and it flies free. Towing a hang glider can stress it beyond its design limits and may result in disaster. Most of the kites designed for towing, and manufactured for this purpose alone, are smaller and more heavily built. A hang glider is larger and lighter, which enables it to capture the wind and soar.

The most common and popular, as well as the least expensive, of the modern hang gliders is the flexible Rogallo shape. This V-shaped craft, with two leading tubular edges, a keel down the center, and a cross member to stiffen it, is an ultralight, foot-launched, tailless glider. It flies in the same manner and is subject to the same aerodynamic laws as any other aircraft operating with its engine off.

A hang glider gets "lift" from the relative motion of the air over its wing and experiences "drag," or wind resistance, just like any aircraft. All hang gliders use gravity as their motivating force: The act of falling is what makes the glider fly.

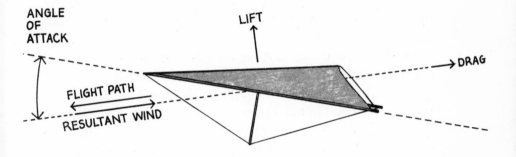

Lift and drag are aerodynamic forces. They result from an aircraft's motion through the air. The glider doesn't care how fast it is moving over the ground since its performance is directly related to air speed. Drag is a force any object experiences when it is in motion through the air. Also, a wing producing lift incurs additional drag due to that lift. Lift is produced by placing the wing at an angle of attack to the airstream.

The difference between a hang glider and any other type of controlled glider is the method in which it is guided. Most enclosed gliders have controls similar to those of airplanes: The pilot moves a stick and kicks rudders to steer the aircraft.

A hang glider uses the principle of shifting weight, which moves the center of gravity, to control the balance of forces (lift and drag) in flight.

With precise moves and careful shifts of the body over the control bar, the hang glider can be made to hover in one spot. Pete Brock once flew off the popular cliffs of Torrance Beach in California and found a perfect updraft. He slowed his hang glider and, relative to the ground, stopped.

A sea gull flew over to investigate, and it, too, stopped to hover a few feet away.

"He came alongside as I was hovering. Neither of us moved," said Brock. "We were side by side, studying each other. There wasn't a sound. I could see the slightest motion of the feathers at the end of his wings as he trimmed. I was thrilled."

Finally, each satisfied with the inspection of the other, Brock shifted his weight and soared off as the gull glided away in the opposite direction.

Vallé, Brock, Albiston, and many of the other record holders and experienced fliers you will read about are young, dynamic men. Who *else* can fly a hang glider?

The fact is, almost anyone can fly a hang glider. Perhaps

Photo opposite page: A hang glider pilot uses the principle of shifting weight (thus the center of gravity) to steer the glider. This pilot is going to turn right, believe it or not.

not as far or as long, it is true, but anyone with the physical strength to handle a glider on the ground can fly one. If you want to fly, you *can* fly. No license is required since, according to regulatory agencies such as the Federal Aviation Administration, a hang glider is only "making temporary use" of the air. Altitude is seldom more than a couple of hundred feet. Many hang gliders are only "ground-skimmed" throughout the careers of their pilots, with the flier maneuvering the craft over low rolling terrain or sand dunes.

If you find that you do not have the strength to handle a glider on the ground as the wind increases, then you should not fly it. The wind and the ground handling are the limiting factors.

Almost all pilots, as they become more skilled, learn that a heavier wind can *help* ground-handling. They learn to "fly" the glider up the hill as well as down by lifting on the flying wires and balancing the glider with its nose into the wind. Not only will the glider be weightless if this is done correctly, but it can actually help propel the pilot back up the hill.

Is age a limiting factor in hang gliding? There are hang gliding pilots, many of them expert, in their early teens. At the other end, a grandmother of eighty, perhaps the oldest person ever to hang glide, tried the sport at Playa del Ray, in California. She flew off a low sand hill for a beach landing.

"It was so exciting; oh, it was just grand, simply wonderful," she said enthusiastically after her first flight. Would she ever try a second flight? "As soon as the glider is fixed, I'm going to go again," she promised. The glider had been bent by her son, a skilled hang glider on a subsequent flight.

Hang gliding has grown so in popularity that there is

hardly a place in the country where someone has not attempted it. The most popular areas are those where conditions allow a pilot to take off and fly for a period of time in safety, then land with the same safety. These areas often have low rolling hills where the glider seldom gets more than a dozen or so feet off the ground and where the pilot can ground-skim to his heart's content. Steady breezes and a takeoff point are all that are necessary.

"Mountain flying" is also very popular with experienced hang gliders. The glider is carried to the top of the mountain; after it is assembled, it is flown into the valley. Long flights are very possible if the wind is right, and flights of five or ten minutes are quite common under these conditions.

Coastlines offer beach cliffs for flying and soft sand for landing. At mountains or beaches, the wind up the face of the cliff can hold a hang glider in the air for hours until the pilot is ready to land. Then he merely shifts his weight, pulls back slightly on the control bar, and glides down to the landing point he has selected.

Hang gliders are noted for their ingenuity in finding new places to fly. One hang glider flew off a big-city skyscraper, but this is a very dangerous stunt and is *not* recommended. Hang gliders in the Midwest have learned that "silo and grain elevator flying" is great fun, and an abandoned railroad bridge near Flagstaff, Arizona, has become a popular hang gliding site for pilots from that area. They glide off the trestle and land in a dry riverbed.

Your state has many flying sites, some of them probably very near your area, so go out and take a look.

But is hang gliding a truly *safe* sport?

Yes!

...And no.

Yes, if you are trained before you fly and fly according to the rules which every sport must have. No, if you are a cowboy flier. People have been killed hang gliding, more than most hang gliders like to admit, and many more have been injured. But each accident can be attributed to pilot error, stunting beyond the design limits of the glider, attempting acrobatic maneuvers beyond the skill of the pilot, mistakes in reading the wind and weather, and the like.

There is a popular hang gliding area in Southern California called Escape Country. This is a sportsman's hangout where motorcycling, skydiving, and other sports are enjoyed. The owner of Escape Country, Jim Robinson, was reluctant to allow hang gliders on the property even though a fine series of gradually heightening takeoff points were available and winds were almost perfect.

Finally, Robinson tried hang gliding himself.

"The people who say it is dangerous haven't tried it," he explained to a newspaper reporter later. "It is really a matter of being afraid of what you're not familiar with. We had some parachutists here and they thought the hang gliders were nuts. Any action sport has a certain amount of danger. But most accidents are pilot error. Guys without safety devices trying to do loops and jumping off hills beyond their ability."

Needless to say, with Robinson hooked on the sport, Escape Country was opened to hang gliding.

Still, it is a high-risk sport, and some continue to question the logic of participating in something when the result of failure can be so serious. In one case there were high-voltage wires near the landing area of a popular gliding spot near Malibu, California. There had never been an accident. Regulars warned newcomers right away of the danger, even though you had to really stretch your flight to get to the wires.

One young hang glider flying off this spot for the first time forgot the warnings. He overshot the landing area, hit the wires, and was electrocuted. That's one of the reasons experienced hang glider pilots stress safety so strongly. They know that hang gliding is such an exhilarating experience that a pilot unfamiliar with the territory can forget warnings. He enjoys himself so much over a new spot that he becomes a sightseer and wants to see it all in the first flight.

Another incident occurred at Sylmar, California, site of the famous 1971 earthquake. Major hang gliding contests are held here from a high takeoff point over rugged shelves and rocks.

Flying weather was near perfect, with fifteen-minute flights the rule rather than the exception. A group of pilots broke down their gliders, hauled them to the top by truck, and assembled them. Then, one by one, they glided off the 2,400-foot summit.

While the first four or five were in the air, the last two got ready. After takeoff, both flew into a sudden "rotor," an uncontrolled column of wild air found near cliff faces. The two gliders crashed on a level spot a dozen feet below the top. One flier suffered injuries and had to be brought back down by truck. Although bloodied, he was unbowed and would have flown again that day if his glider had not been damaged. The other pilot managed to take off from the crash site and complete his flight.

Neither man had received any warning. But both admitted that had they been more experienced or more careful, they would have avoided the rotor by changing their takeoff point. Meanwhile, though some crashes have been worse than these, thousands of flights have been made off Sylmar without mishap.

To hang glider pilots, flying is much more than stuffing yourself into a huge machine with stewardesses serving drinks while you streak from one city to another. Flying a hang glider is basic and pure. Even some airline pilots enjoy taking a busman's holiday by hang gliding on their days off. Such flying embodies the true wonder of flight and hang gliding is probably as close as man will ever come to "flying like a bird."

2 / A LITTLE HISTORY

The most basic form of flight known to man is that of riding without power on currents of air. Men have dreamed of such flight from the beginning of time. Doubtless there was a caveman who imagined the wonder of being able to fly like the great pterodactyl. If not for pure recreation, then certainly he considered how much easier it would be to hunt or to protect himself if he could fly.

According to legend, it was the father of Icarus, Daedalus, who envisioned man flying like a bird. Held in exile on the island of Crete and longing once again to see his home in Athens, Daedalus knew King Minos would never permit him to travel by land or by sea. He was a prisoner.

But the air, decided Daedalus, was free to every man. So he studied the flight of birds and began to affix feathers to small flying devices. He followed the patterns of feathers in

27

the wings of the birds. His son, Icarus, watched with anticipation.

Finally, Daedalus fashioned a man-sized set of wings which he could flap with his arms to suspend himself in the air. He built another set for his son.

"I advise you," said Daedalus to his impatient young son, "to remain halfway between the waves, lest they, should you go too low, make your wings heavy, and the sun, lest it burn you with its fires should you go too high.

"Take me as your guide to follow," he said, finishing the world's first ground school lecture. Then he kissed his son for a final time.

Flapping his arms, Daedalus flew into the air. Icarus followed. Some fishermen, shepherds, and farmers below were dumbfounded when they saw these humans flying in the sky. The two passed the island of Samos, then Juno, Delos, and Paros. They could see Lebinthos and Calymna, and Icarus' joy knew no bounds. He swept up higher and higher, abandoning his father and his father's warnings.

He wanted to reach the sun.

But the wax holding the feathers to the framework on his arms began to melt, and the feathers, one by one, dropped away. Daedalus tried to shout a warning to his soaring son, but the boy couldn't hear.

Finally, the legend goes, Icarus was beating his naked arms and falling, falling into the sea far below. His mouth screamed his father's name as he plunged into the cold water.

Old Daedalus cursed his invention as he searched for the body of his only son.

Unfortunately, there is a strong similarity, even to the

crash, between young Icarus and certain hang glider pilots today. The exhilaration of flying on the wind does affect the judgment of some young pilots who will not temper their joy with cool and calm analysis and safe and sane flight.

Leonardo da Vinci conceived a mechanical wing for a man and drew plans for it during the early sixteenth century. The wing was to be powered by leg muscles, for as Da Vinci said, "Man has more strength in his legs than is needed by his weight alone."

Perhaps fortunately, there is no record of anyone's having actually tested his wing. The Da Vinci parachute might have succeeded, and his helicopter model might really have flown, but a man simply cannot fly by beating his arms or legs.

Why not? A bird can do it, and a man has more strength than a bird. For one thing, a bird's heart beats much faster than a man's, and the breathing cycle of a bird is more rapid. Oxygen is pumped through a bird's body much faster. Therefore, a bird, ounce for ounce, has much more strength and energy than a man. As John Taylor wrote, "The human body cannot possibly compete with such highly geared machines."

But man *can* fly on the wind with wings.

An Englishman followed the general lead of Da Vinci three centuries later. Sir George Cayley perfected the idea of the "airfoil," the shape which gives a wing its lift. In 1809 he laid down the principles for heavier-than-air flight after building numerous gliders with kite wings and cross-shaped tails. His gliders were the first to exhibit "dihedral," the turning up of the ends of the wings to increase stability.

Louis Pierre Mouillard, of Egypt, published one of the classics of aeronautical engineering in 1881. His *L'Empire de l'air* is still a valuable discussion of flight. Meanwhile, in 1871, the famous Otto Lilienthal became interested in flight and began to work on gliders. Before he died in 1896, he had made more than 2,000 flights, some to more than 1,000 feet and as fast as 22 miles per hour. Lilienthal studied curved wing surfaces, monoplane and biplane construction, and control surfaces, and in 1896 he developed a 2¼ horsepower carbonic motor weighing 88 pounds for propelling his flight.

But he never had a chance to test the motor, for during a practice session of one of his gliders he lost control and fell to the ground from 50 feet. He was carried to his bed with a broken back.

The next morning he smiled up at close friends and said (according to which historian you believe), "This was the price of progress," or, "Sacrifices must be made." Then Lilienthal died.

It is possible that the work of Lilienthal inspired the Wright brothers, but more likely it was the pioneer gliding flights of Octave Chanute. Chanute made his flights at Dune Park, Illinois, on the shore of Lake Michigan.

Chanute summed up all the aeronautical knowledge to date in 1894 in a book entitled *Progress in Flying Machines*, a work which included much on Lilienthal. Since Chanute was a wealthy man, he was able to play with the idea of flight. He also made money available to others for study, likely among them the Wright brothers. He is known to have corresponded with them over an extended period of time and visited them in Ohio.

Meanwhile, men like John Montgomery and Daniel Maloney were experimenting with manned powerless flight.

Both Montgomery and Maloney were killed at the controls of gliders that crashed.

It was finally Wilbur and Orville Wright who made the original "giant leap for mankind" from hang gliding to powered flight. The brothers had worked for several years on the possibility of flight. From 1900 to 1903 they conducted many serious flight experiments at their "summer camp," a hot, sticky, mosquito-ridden sand dune area at Kitty Hawk, North Carolina.

These were hang gliding experiments with different sizes and styles of wings, experiments which ultimately led to the first true airplane patent being applied for and granted in 1903.

At that point hang gliding activity, which had only been a means to an end, diminished. The point of flying was now to get from one place to another as quickly as possible, not just to glide about for enjoyment.

The objective of Francis M. Rogallo, an employee of the Langley Research Center, in Virginia, and the "father" of modern hang gliding, was to devise a wing that could be easily folded into the sides of an aircraft and then, when deployed, allow the aircraft to float safely back to earth. Finally Rogallo's idea of a limp delta-shaped parawing was presented to the National Aeronautics and Space Administration as a possible means for the reentry of a space vehicle. Meanwhile, Rogallo had obtained more than twenty patents covering the parawing.

Although the idea was rejected as a reentry device, the Army used the parawing design for a steerable parachute, a design that was quickly picked up by sport parachutists.

From 1941 to the 1960s Americans like Volmer Johnson,

The "Australian Birdman," Bill Bennett, takes off from Dante's View in Death Valley for a record making flight of 6.2 miles to the valley floor, 5,757 feet below.

Dave Kilbourne, and Richard Miller were experimenting with home-built Rogallo-shaped gliders and different launch techniques. Rogallo's parawing was also rejuvenated as a device to be towed behind a boat to lift a water-skier into the air. "Kiting" with the Rogallo wing became quite popular, especially after Bill Moyes and Bill "The Australian Birdman" Bennett (a prominent manufacturer of hang gliders and towed kites) introduced the idea to American sportsmen. Bennett, who has captivated audiences at ski shows across the country and has flown over both the Statue of Liberty and the Golden Gate Bridge, introduced the modern swing-seat method of suspending the pilot beneath the glider and the trapeze bar to control direction and altitude. Before that, pilots used the parallel-bar arrangement, from which they literally swung by their armpits.

Towing diminished in popularity in 1971, when a hang glider was prominently foot-launched by Dave Kilbourne and the sport began in its modern form. But the glider is still not in its final form. Manufacturers are experimenting with swallowtail shapes and other gradual design changes to make gliders safer and more responsive and, for some gliders, more competitive in distance, maneuverability, speed, or whatever "high performance" is required.

The basic Rogallo shape is still considered the safest, most conventional hang glider for beginning or leisure fliers, although strange and wondrous gliders are seen every weekend at most of the gliding sites in the United States.

Moorpark, in California, is an intermediate training site: not for beginners and yet too modest for experts. One day pilots there were enjoying what for that area were considered long flights. Since the site has a mildly steep hill of perhaps 150 feet and the winds were relatively calm that day, flights of 30 or 40 seconds were about normal. One pilot caught a good wind and was cheered for a flight of nearly one minute as he sailed over the pilots' parking lot to land well beyond the point where most of the other gliders were touching down.

Then an Icarus glider arrived in its odd flat trailer. Rigid-wing hang gliders do not break down as conveniently as Rogallos. They are large and cumbersome, and on the ground they appear to be much too thick and heavy for any flight, especially foot-launched soaring.

It took the pilot nearly half an hour to assemble the glider, and he needed the help of three others to get it up the hill. Finally it was launched from Moorpark's gentle slope.

The glider seemed to defy gravity. Pilots learn very early in the sport that the glide ratio of a rigid wing is considerably higher than that of a Rogallo shape, and this glider was proving it. It soared out away from the top of the hill in almost a straight line; then the pilot began to bank it very gently. Back and forth across the face of the hill went the wing, ever so gradually sinking. The flight time was at least four times that of the best of the others.

Perhaps tomorrow, or the next day, a manufacturer of hang gliders will come up with even more efficient style. The shape might be completely different from those that are now available, or more likely, it will be a small technical change in today's design. And the glide ratio will increase once again.

Photo opposite page: The "Icarus" glider has a better glide ratio than the standard Rogallo shape.

Gliders come in a variety of beautiful colors and designs. Here the "Casper the Ghost" glider of pilot George Barker comes in for a landing at Sylmar.

The sport continues to grow and change. Like the barn-stormers of old, some pilots will allow all comers, for a fee, to try their glider after a few minutes of ground school. This type of flying is *not* recommended. Just remember that unlike the old barnstormers, in this case it is you, not him, taking the chance.

There are however, dual hang gliders in which an experienced pilot can take along a passenger or an instructor can teach a student while flying.

Today's hang gliders come in a variety of colors that are beautiful to behold. Lovely butterfly patterns and colors of every rainbow hue dot the sky at popular hang gliding areas. Manufacturers who have settled on a standard, safe, conventional shape now vie with each other by producing more and more colorful sail designs, and hang gliding has become so popular that most manufacturers today are unable to keep up with the orders.

3/GLIDER CONSTRUCTION

There is a great difference between the hang gliders of the past and near past and the hang gliders of today. Until quite recently, it was not uncommon to see strange lash-ups of plastic bamboo, hardware store bolts, baling wire, and even *tape* at hang gliding areas. With a great flapping of plastic and bending of spars and leading edges, the pioneers would run and throw themselves off hills and cliffs.

Most often these constructions would fly, though not nearly as well as the carefully designed gliders now available. But fly they did, and the sport grew.

Occasionally, though, they did not fly, or they became uncontrollable in a tricky wind. Hang glider pilots were injured. Some were killed. As late as 1974, more than three dozen deaths were attributed to the sport of hang gliding.

Only recently, at a popular hang gliding area in the Midwest, a great black and aluminum glider arrived. It was obviously homemade by the young pilot preparing to fly it. He straightened cables and tightened bolts, and gradually the glider took shape. The sail sagged and the spars were bent and bowed by the cables, but he struggled up the hill with his flying machine. Activity among the others stopped as more and more pilots turned to watch the young man with the black glider.

He walked carefully to the edge of the hill, tilted his glider forward on its nose to park it momentarily, and strapped himself into his prone harness. Then he lifted the glider, leveled it, waited a few seconds for the wind to be right, and stepped off.

The glider *flew*. It didn't fly well, and it flew with a great deal of noise from the flapping of the loose plastic, which actually appeared to be a number of heavy-duty trash bags fastened together. The pilot brought the glider to the ground with a flourish near an attentive group of other pilots. He stalled very precisely and touched down.

Now, hang glider pilots are typically easygoing, helpful, and friendly sportsmen. They are noted for vocally applauding the good flight of another pilot, and they'll stop their own fun to chat with a newcomer and exchange notes on the sport. But although they should have cheered this flight, they began to shout in derision. Instead of congratulating the young man for his resource in building a glider from scratch, they laughed and made obvious remarks about "garbage bag" flying.

Hang gliding has passed through the homemade stage, the stage that injured and killed so many fine young pilots. But enthusiasts are now very concerned, even uptight, about safety. They are the first to acknowledge that their sport is only as safe as their equipment and their intelligence. They are never enthusiastic about unsafe equipment, which might cause injuries or deaths and ultimately be responsible for closing flying areas.

Not that you can't pull together fifteen or twenty dollars' worth of television antenna poles, plastic, and wire, then hang it together with some hardware store nuts and bolts. Hang gliding is not regulated, except by its own participants. They want it to stay that way, so they tend to be unpleasant toward people who might hurt themselves and, in so doing, hurt the sport.

One young man crashed after attempting to fly an obviously unsafe homemade glider, and for a period of time he was paralyzed from the waist down because of injuries to his spine. A few close friends visited him to cheer him up, but most of the pilots from the area wrote letters to hang gliding publications and commented to newspaper reporters on his lack of intelligence for even attempting to fly the homemade glider.

Home-built gliders are discouraged for anyone but the most experienced pilots who are involved with glider research and development. These pilots understand the risks and are willing to gamble to advance the sport.

Glider kits have been very popular over the years. They come as unassembled and, in some cases, uncut and undrilled batches of supplies from hang glider manufacturers. You receive good aircraft-standard parts, but it's up to you to drill the holes and assemble the glider.

Certainly these are less expensive than factory-built gliders. However, very few manufacturers provide the unfinished kit anymore. Too many things can go wrong when a novice is required to drill, splice, and reinforce parts, swage cables, mount sails, and then assemble.

According to Gary Vallé, if there is any place for the application of "Murphy's Law" ("If anything can go wrong, it will, and at the worst possible time"), it is in a sport in which construction must be exact or disaster may result.

Gary remembered a telephone call one manufacturer received from an angry customer after the young man had purchased an unfinished glider kit.

"It simply won't fly," complained the customer. "I did everything according to the plans, and still I'm lucky I haven't broken my legs. Every time I try to fly it off the hill, it tries to *turn around*."

As it turned out, the young man had installed the harness the wrong way and had been trying to take off backwards!

There are also manufacturers who will provide a "finished" kit. This is a box containing the necessary parts with all the factory work completed except assembly. The spars are cut to the exact length and drilled in the right places, and the cables are cut and swaged precisely. The customer must bolt the leading edges and keel to the nose plate, a reasonably simple job that can hardly go wrong.

But installing the sail is a job that *can* go wrong, for orienting and tensioning the sail constitute a science. If not done correctly, the glider might still fly, but it might not fly as it should. The pilot may never get the best the glider can give if the glider has not been factory-tuned and test-flown by an expert.

Roughly speaking, for prices do vary, there is about a hundred-dollar difference in cost between a finished kit and a factory-built glider. The Hang Glider Manufacturers Association, a group who have banded together to standardize and improve the safety of gliders, are generally opposed to unfinished kits. They tolerate finished kits, which some of their members provide to customers, but they strongly recommend factory-built models. These can cost from about $500 to $1,500, depending on size, which depends on pilot weight. The HGMA won't even talk about homemade gliders. Finished kits, though not factory-tuned or flight-tested, can be a good buy for an experienced hang glider only.

Some dealers obtain factory-finished kits from the manufacturers, then assemble them at the dealership and sell them as factory-built. This is not hazardous, provided they are flight-tested by an expert before customers pick them up. The whole idea of kits is to save money. And if the dealership wants to build the glider and the customer wants to save the time of building it and pay the price, why not?

Homemade? Factory-unfinished or -finished? The best way to go is with a factory-finished and test-flown glider. Unlike many other manufacturing processes, where a *sample number* of the finished product go to the testing department, every glider from a reputable manufacturer is test-flown. You will know that your own glider has been flown at least once by an expert before you pick it up.

This is what you will get when you purchase your glider: two leading edges, a keel, and a crossbar to hold the other items in place, all made of aircraft-standard, drawn (not extruded) aluminum tubing. Under this framework will be a drawn aluminum control bar, and over it a drawn aluminum kingpost. Aircraft-quality stainless-steel-coated cables hold the unit together in the right shape.

The sail is made of a special type of Dacron that will not stretch or change shape during flight. Nylon and other plastics have a tendency to deform under load, ruining the flight

characteristics of the glider. Polyethylene was the mainstay of early-day hang gliders, and it is low in cost. It should not be used, however, because it does tend to tear. As you soar off a mountaintop, the last thing you want to hear from overhead is a tiny *rrrrrrrip!*

Aircraft-standard stainless-steel nuts, bolts, and other hardware are used throughout the hang glider and should be used when replacing a part. Occasionally a glider will land a little harder than usual and bend a bolt, weakening it. But no experienced hang glider pilot would go to the local hardware store to buy a replacement unless the store handled stainless-steel parts. The pilot's life depends on the solidarity of construction of his glider, so buying cheap parts is folly.

There is also a suspension sling to which the harness of the pilot is attached. Modern manufacturers use the highest-quality mountaineering material, since mountaineers also trust their lives to these triple-sewn safety straps. In quality gliders the mounting brackets that hold all these parts together are made of stainless steel.

The suspension system supports the weight of the pilot and leaves his hands free to control the glider. There are two popular suspension systems from which to choose: the swing seat and the prone harness.

The swing seat is the less expensive and perhaps the less complicated. The glider is flown with the pilot in a sitting position. The seat, with a safety belt to hold the pilot in place, swings from the suspension sling attached to the kite at the top of the control bar. Before the pilot runs to take off,

Photo opposite page: Every glider from every manufacturer should be test flown before sale.

the seat is strapped to his backside; then, when the glider becomes airborne, he just sits down.

The more popular flying position is the prone. The prone harness allows the pilot to lie flat beneath the glider, his hands free to move the control bar. To help hold his legs out behind him, the harness can be equipped with extra hangers that go around the knees and attach to the sling. As the glider lifts off the ground, the pilot just lies out flat in his harness. For long-distance flying the harness is often equipped with sheepskin padding to prevent chafing and cutting.

Both the swing seat and the prone harness permit the pilot to shift his body under the glider, which changes the center of gravity and allows him to steer the craft right, left, up, or down.

Specially designed helmets are also available from most manufacturers. Lightweight, yet built to every existing safety standard, they have open earholes so the pilot can hear the wind in the sail for better control, and they are strongly recommended by every hang gliding instructor and school.

Finally, since hang gliders are often carried in folded position on the top of a car or truck, carrying bags are available to protect them from the weather.

Selecting a hang glider for yourself is a rather complicated process. It should be done only after initial instruction so you are certain of exactly what you want. Basically, the size and shape are determined by the load the glider is to carry and the job it is to do. A pilot who wishes to soar on weekends off the cliffs of the local beach or over the local rolling hills will choose a glider different from that of the pilot who wishes to compete on a tight slalom course with pinpoint landing requirements. There are standard and high-performance

Rogallo gliders available and, of course, a wide number of rigid-wing styles and types.

If you are ready for a rigid-wing glider with an airfoil section, an advanced glider with countless variations, you probably already know exactly what you want. You are an experienced pilot, so use your own judgment. The Rogallo-shaped delta-wing glider has fewer design considerations and is more suitable for the conventional sport flier, and shapes are also available for the competition flier.

The leading edges of a delta-shaped glider come together at the front to form an angle that is important to the flight characteristics of the glider. Most new Rogallo gliders have a nose angle (the included angle of the leading edge spars) of about 100° and a sail angle (the included angle of the leading edges of the sail, spread out to its fullest angle and not held by the spars) of about 104°.

Although the sail fits between the spars, it is obviously different from the spars in shape. There is extra sail available, and the amount of extra sail is also very important to the performance of the glider. Called the "billow angle," it is calculated by cutting in half the nose angle, cutting in half the sail angle, then subtracting the former from the latter. A standard Rogallo has a billow angle of about 2°.

$$
\begin{array}{lll}
100° \text{ (nose angle)} & 104° \text{ (sail angle)} & 52° \\
\div\ 2 & \div\ 2 & -50° \\
\hline
50° & 52° & 2° \text{ (billow angle)}
\end{array}
$$

So remember these important angle measurements for a hang glider: standard nose angle about 100°; standard sail angle about 102°; and standard billow angle of about 2°.

This Skytrek Rogallo shape glider has a nose angle of 90°.

The billow angle on a high-performance glider is smaller than that on a standard glider. In fact, the normal way to increase the performance of a glider is to decrease the billow angle, but you must trade off control. The higher the performance, the more critical the control.

Some delta-wing nose angles run to as much as 120°, with a correspondingly high sail angle. Again generally speaking, the greater the nose angle, the greater the sail area, and thus, the greater the lift. The smaller the nose angle, the smaller the sail area, resulting in less lift but greater speed and stability.

Hang glider design is a complicated science of angles, lift, drag and glide ratios, and other technical points. Fortunately for the novice, the manufacturers understand these technical matters and incorporate them into their basic products.

Rogallo-type hang gliders are generally referred to by the size of their lead spars, not by "wing span" as with other aircraft. Since the included angle between the lead spars is far more important than the width of the glider, the spar length is the measurement. Following is a chart giving standard hang glider sizes for pilot weights to be carried.

Pilot weight (IN POUNDS)	Glider size (IN FEET)
100–135	16
135–155	17
155–180	18
180–205	19
205–225	20

Some companies make smaller gliders on special order for lighter pilots, and most will custom-make a glider for a pilot who weighs more than 225 pounds. Remember, though, that these are general figures. A kite too large for you can be slow and difficult to handle. One too small for you can be too fast and responsive for good control. The most modern gliders are high-performance types. The square-foot area of the sail can be reduced with the latest shapes. Your hang glider dealer will advise you according to your size, skill, and area of flight.

4 / INSTRUCTION

Let's get one thing straight. There is only *one* way to learn to hang glide, and that is with competent formal instruction from a recommended hang gliding school.

No, you do not *have* to go to a school. It is true that every day some fledgling pilots are being instructed by buddies, but the day of the "two-minute ground school" should be over forever.

One young lady proudly watched her boyfriend, no more than an intermediate flier himself, as he practiced at an East Coast location. Then she turned to some onlookers, a warm, loving glow on her face.

"Bill is going to teach me himself, once he gets the hang of it," she said. "He doesn't trust anyone else to do it."

Sad, for throughout the country there are schools to teach the novice how to hang glide safely and skillfully. Just like surfing and skin diving, hang gliding went through a period of "learning from your pals." The novice *had* to learn on the cliff's edge with the cold wind in his face because that was the only place available to learn.

Recently, at a beach in Oregon, a doctor who had decided to learn from one of his patients was strapped into a harness and led to the edge of the hill. It was a small hill, but still forty or fifty feet high. With a few words of caution and wisdom, and some joking about "when I get him on the table, I'll get even," the doctor was told to run for the edge.

He did, and seconds later was spitting out a mouthful of sand, which anywhere else could have been hard rocks. Four times he tried, until finally he got the idea of guiding the glider up and down. How much easier it would have been for him if he had been able to try out the harness and sling in one of the simulators now being used in hang gliding schools.

Some of the "old-timers"—those involved in the sport for more than a couple of years—still insist that the only way to learn is on the front lines, at the edge of a cliff with a stiff wind blowing in your face. But *don't* you believe them. That's nature's way, where only the strongest survive, and you might be *second* strongest that day. Get your training from a training school.

An example of a good gliding school is the Southern California School of Hang Gliding. The instructors are Rich Grigsby and Mike Addison, both skilled hang glider pilots and instructors. Grigsby was an NCAA gymnastics champion and a professional trapeze artist, so he knows flying.

As a beginner you report to the class, sign a release form, and settle in for three hours of "ground school." During this

Author Ross R. Olney watches as instructor Mike Addison demonstrates
the school simulator.

The best way to learn is to go to school. This pretty young student is in good hands with skilled pilots Trip Mellinger (left) and Joe Greblo (right).

time you see films on hang gliding, watch a glider being set up, and listen to lectures on safety, weather, and other technical matters. You then "fly" a simulator, which gives you an accurate feel of what it will be like suspended under the glider.

The instructor can make the simulator stall, dive, or bank the wrong way. Until you are able to correct these conditions, you go no further in your training.

After ground school comes flight school. It is possible to fail the ground phase and have to go through again, but most pass easily. You go to the flight training area, a beginner hill, and with other students you help to set up a glider or two. Now you understand all the aluminum poles and wires and clips. You know a kingpost from a keel, and you know how to step into your own harness.

Yet no student pushes to be first. So the instructor gives you a chance at ground handling the glider under flight conditions. It seems big and clumsy until you learn how to get assistance, rather than problems, from the wind. No one notices that the group is moving closer and closer to the edge and that every one is gradually being harnessed and helmeted and made ready. The instructor points to . . . to *you*. The time has come.

So you do it, and it works just fine, just as he promised it would. If one or two of you skim in a little hard or stall a little high and parachute down, none is scratched, and everyone enjoys the momentary confusion. You are *hang gliders*.

But you are not yet ready for the cliffs. You must practice

One of the high points of the author's research was this very first hang gliding flight off a "bunny hill" at Redondo Beach in California.

and practice, gradually working your way up, perfecting your skills as you go. Eventually you will be able to take on the intermediate slopes.

Some schools, when they move novices from the bunny hills to hills the instructor can no longer run up and down, use citizens' band radios to instruct. The student wears a headset in his helmet or a small speaker is mounted on the glider. The instructor watches the flight and advises the student as he is flying.

At a good school you'll learn the exact procedure for setting up a hang glider. They'll teach you to do the following:

1. Rotate the control bar downward and stand the glider into the wind on its control bar and nose plate.

2. Attach the rear flying (bottom) wires to the keel. Be certain when attaching wires that cables and brackets are not twisted.

3. Connect the kingpost to the keel wire.

4. Spread the crossbar.

5. Spread the leading edges, one at a time, and join them to the crossbar. Also join the kingpost side wires to the crossbar at this time. Be sure to get the saddles between crossbar, keel, and brackets in the correct order.

6. Be sure all cable ends are properly oriented in their tangs and on the flying wire shackles.

7. Tighten the kingpost wire turnbuckles so both the top and bottom cables are just taut, not too tight or too loose, with no more than about three threads showing outside the turnbuckle end. Tightening the top kingpost wire by its turnbuckle will, of course, pull on and tighten the bottom

flying wires, though they themselves have no turnbuckle. The kingpost wires may be less taut in flight since the flying wires take the load.

8. Check the keel—the middle spar—to see if it sweeps upward from the level of the leading edges. This 1½- to 2-inch upward bend is called "reflex" and is the source for pitch stability in a Rogallo. Never fly the glider unless this reflex is evident.

9. Be sure the keel isn't bent to one side or the other because of a twisted cable end.

10. Check your own harness carefully to be certain it is on correctly.

Once you have set up the glider, the instructor will teach you to give your glider a complete preflight check, following this list:

1. All nuts and bolts are fully tightened.

2. Both turnbuckles have no more than three threads showing.

3. Safety pins secure cleavis pins.

4. There are no bent bolts, since bent bolts are substantially weakened.

5. The pilot suspension web is in perfect condition.

6. Cables are not frayed or damaged.

7. Cables are taut, but not overly taut.

8. The keel spar is straight but with an upward reflex.

9. The keel and leading edge rivets securing the sail are not tearing out.

10. The keel, leading edges, and crossbar are not bent.

Gary Vallé demonstrates glider set up. Above: He has rotated the control bar downward, aimed the glider into the wind, and he is attaching the bottom (flying) wires. Below: Vallé attaches the kingpost to keel wire.

Above: Vallé spreads the leading edges and joins them to the crossbar.
Below: He checks his own harness, helmet, and the weather and wind
before flight. Right: Once the glider and harness have been checked out, he
is ready to fly!

11. Locknuts are locking, not worn out.
12. Flying wire shackles are free to rotate.
13. Wing nuts are secured with safety pins.

In addition, the glider should be inspected regularly, and especially after *every* hard landing, for the following:

1. Bent bolts.
2. Cracked saddles.
3. Damage to control bar bracket.
4. Holes in the sail (which, of course, can be repaired, though major repairs should be done by an expert).
5. Security of pop rivets on leading edge and keel splicing sleeves (if spliced).
6. Security of pop rivets on trim bracket.
7. Straightness of leading edges, keel, and crossbar.

At the flying site you will probably get some final lectures about wind and weather, perhaps while everyone is resting between flights. One of the great beauties of hang gliding is the cooperation and understanding developed between the pilot and nature. It is the air which supports the pilot and his craft, nothing else. And wherever you may fly after this basic training, you will always work with nature, learning to take advantage of its smiles and to beware of its whims and caprices.

You must become very familiar with wind direction and speed. This is one of the first things you must learn as a gliding pilot—and also one of the most difficult.

At most flying sites there are wind socks to indicate wind direction and force. After you have arrived at the site, tested the wind, and set up the glider at the launch point, check the wind once again. If it has substantially increased, or increased beyond the point where you feel perfectly comfortable flying, *put your glider away* so you can fly another day. Pilot error accounts for almost every hang gliding accident, and reading the wind incorrectly is one of the most common pilot errors.

Yet even worse than reading the wind incorrectly is not paying attention to your reading when it tells you the wind is too strong.

The following is a guide for reading the force of the wind:

• If leaves and small pieces of paper and other debris are in motion, if small flags are being rippled but not moved out away from the pole, if water shows motion from the wind, if the wind is strong enough to turn a wind direction indicator— the wind is up to about *10 miles per hour.*

• If dust and loose paper are being blown about, the branches of small trees are being moved, if the water is beginning to show small whitecaps—the wind is moving at about *11 to 18 miles per hour.*

• If small trees are beginning to sway and the branches of larger trees are beginning to move, if the wind is making a sound through the trees and brush, if whitecaps are beginning to appear on small bodies of water, if the wind can be felt solidly against the face—it is moving at about *18 to 25 miles per hour.*

• If the branches of large trees are swaying, if the wind is whistling through the branches and wires and antennas, if the sail on your glider pops and bangs during ground handling—the wind is probably *more than 25 miles per hour.*

During ground school and again at the flying site you will learn about the different types of air movement that assist the hang glider who understands them. Some pilots fly at locations having only one type of air movement; others will encounter different types of movement within their flying territories.

THERMALS.   Everyone knows that heated air rises. Thermals are masses of heated air rising rapidly. The thermal occurs in a column shape, a huge tube of air shooting skyward. If a hang glider flies into a thermal, the nose will instantly pitch up and the glider will begin to rise rapidly. Just as quickly, the glider may move out of the thermal and once again float on a smooth and level course.

Many experienced pilots attempt to use thermals to maintain flight. They seek out and enter them. Then, to remain in the thermal and continue to gain altitude, they circle slowly. The pilots watch birds or columns of dust to find the thermal and to determine its limits and force. Endurance records have been set by pilots familiar with using thermals, and any pilot's flight can be extended several times over once he learns the secrets of thermals and how to find them.

CONVECTION CURRENTS.   Ground surfaces such as sand, rocks, barren land, and plowed ground give off heat into the air directly above them. Water, vegetation, trees, and brushland tend to retain heat. This uneven heating of air causes heat waves to rise somewhat faster in some areas than in others. A pilot flying over terrain composed of different surfaces will be affected by these convection currents. His flight path will be wavy rather than straight. He will gently rise and fall as he progresses. At first the nose of the glider will gradually pitch up; then it will descend gently. Experienced hang glider pilots make use of these currents to maintain flight. They seek out the areas where the air is rising and attempt to avoid the areas where it is not. Most hang gliding sites have their own best flight paths that take advantage of local convection currents. To learn these flight paths, watch the experts fly, and follow their lead.

DEFLECTED AIR. If you have ever watched a candy wrapper blow toward a fence and then suddenly blow over it instead of plastering up against it, you have seen deflected air in action. Air blowing against a surface will travel up the surface and over the top, or around it if possible. It will not just rush up and "stick" there. This holds true against a relatively small object such as a fence as well as a larger one such as a cliff. The air takes the path of least resistance to get over or around, just as water does.

Hang glider pilots take advantage of this air deflection. There are gliding areas where, to take off, the pilot merely stands at the edge of a cliff, usually with a partner to help him hold the nose of the glider. When he is ready, the partner releases the nose and the glider rises on the deflection current of air coming up the face of the cliff.

Where the currents are not that strong, the pilot runs toward the edge of the cliff, and the sail fills with the deflected air as he runs off.

The strength and direction of the wind and the shape and height of the hill determine the strength of the deflection.

An important fact to remember about deflected air is that, like water, it tends to broil and roll and become quite unstable just behind the very edge of the cliff. It rushes up the face, over the top, then rolls back upon itself. A hang glider venturing into this area or allowing himself to be blown into it is going to have to fight for control. For this reason most experienced pilots stay away from the lip of a cliff after taking off.

The learning process in most hang gliding schools will take the novice from bunny hills to areas where he can fly longer but not higher. These might be gently rolling hillocks or sand dunes or other locations where the wind is steady. The beginner gradually works his way to higher locations, learning about glider handling and wind and weather as he goes.

It is not impossible for a beginner to fly off the cliffs of the advanced areas after only a couple lessons. Some of today's experts learned just that way. But others tried and did not survive, so take full advantage of the learning techniques now available.

Remember that a Rogallo-shaped wing has about a 4:1 or, at best, 5:1 glide angle, also known as L/D, or lift to drag, ratio. This is simply the distance the 35- to 45-pound glider will fly forward (4 or 5 feet) for every foot it drops in calm air. Fixed-wing gliders with airfoils have much greater glide ratios, and certain sailplanes have glide ratios of 40:1 or 50:1.

With your knowledge of the L/D ratio you can pick your landing area from your takeoff point, and you should do so before *every* flight.

The landing area should be as large and as flat and as soft as possible. It should be clear of trees, large rocks, wires, houses, or other obstructions. There should also be a clear path between the takeoff area and the landing area. Remember that hang gliders have no right to disturb, disrupt, or endanger people on the ground. This includes picnickers, hikers, and others using their fair share of the outdoors, as you are doing.

Experienced hang gliders make sure there is a wind direction and force indicator in the landing area before they take off. This can be a wind sock or a flag or ribbon, but it should be visible from some distance away so you can prepare and plan your landing.

Land into the wind and then observe the following hang gliding traffic-control courtesies:

1. Get the nose of your glider into the wind, set it down, and unhook your D-ring from the sling. Then walk your glider out of the traffic area as promptly as possible (nose into the wind) so you don't interfere with others trying to land.

2. Carry or walk your glider back up the hill along a path that will not interfere with other fliers coming down.

3. Once you have stepped forward to the takeoff point and checked your harness a final time (to be sure it is solidly hooked to the sling of the glider), take off. You should have preflighted your glider and made all adjustments ahead of time.

4. There is an unwritten rule in hang gliding that you never turn into a hill. If two gliders are approaching each other from opposite directions along a hill or a cliff, the glider that is able to turn *away* from the hill by turning *right* should take the evasive maneuver. The other glider should proceed straight ahead until the possibility of collision has been avoided.

Following is a list of basic flight guidelines for hang glider flying. You will probably learn them in a good school, but just in case you don't. . . .

1. Do not fly under the influence of any substance that will impair your judgment, senses, or vision, including liquor, drugs, or antihistamines.

2. In flight the glider should be kept within a 30° nose-up and 30° nose-down angle from the normal glide attitude and within 60° of the horizon for angle of bank.

3. *Never* fly without a preflight check of your glider, your harness, and yourself. There have been pilots, for example, who have run toward the edge of the cliff, felt the wind pick up the glider at the edge, settled back into their harness for a nice flight, and learned as they tumbled down far beneath their glider that they had forgotten to hitch the harness to the glider sling.

4. Are you too tired, not in good physical condition, or beyond your ability with regard to the wind or area? If so, pack up and quit for the day.

5. Never replace lost parts with hardware store components. Many pilots carry a kit of spare parts of aircraft-quality stainless steel in case something is lost at the flight area. In the excitement of getting the glider ready, it is quite possible to drop a nut or bolt into the brush or sand and lose it.

6. Never improvise a part or component on the spot. One pilot replaced a broken cable with baling wire at the flying site and was fatally injured on the very next flight. If you can't use the correct part or component—though hang glider pilots generally are glad to lend a needed part to a grounded pilot if they have an extra—fold up your glider and enjoy watching the others until the next time.

7. Don't ever pressure or force another pilot, and don't ever allow yourself to be pressured or forced into a flight you

know you shouldn't attempt. Don't try stunts beyond your own skills just because someone else is doing them. That qualifies as pilot error in one of its most glaring forms.

8. Avoid overconfidence. Leave cliff launches and other daring flying to the most experienced fliers.

9. Never hang the pilot suspension web directly from the trim bracket.

10. Always wear a helmet and, in most cases, gloves, too.

11. Know your primary landing spot by inspecting it ahead of time. Have alternate landing areas in your flight path just in case.

12. Be aware of all obstacles in your flight path.

13. Talk to other fliers before flying an area for the first time. They'll be glad to point out any ground rules and special hazards, including capricious winds, at that area.

14. Keep your hands on the control bar at all times during your flight.

15. Always take off and land directly into the wind. Flags or other wind direction indicators are necessary at both points.

16. Never stand on the control bar, and avoid all other foolish stunts. Remember, pilot error causes more injuries than any other factor.

17. Only the most experienced pilots should try 360° turns, and then only after thorough instruction from another expert at that area on the same day. Most pilots take a circle 90° at a time and thus stay out of trouble.

18. Never tow a hang glider behind a boat, car, or other vehicle. Hang gliders are not built to be towed, and design limits can be exceeded.

19. Thoroughly inspect the glider after every hard landing for any damage.

5/THE FAA AND
HANG GLIDING

Motorcycle jumpers, cliff divers, parachutists, and trapeze artists all fly through the air, but they are not regulated by the Federal Aviation Administration. Neither are hang gliding enthusiasts—yet.

You can help keep it that way.

Former FAA Administrator John H. Shaffer, commenting on a commemorative stamp honoring ballooning, said, "The air space over the United States is a national resource belonging to everyone." So far hang gliding has received only recommendations from the FAA, and these are honest, intelligent, and thoughtful.

The great attraction of hang gliding is freedom. It offers everyone the opportunity to move forward at his own pace, to fly with only himself to credit or blame. The picture remains bright. But in view of the long flights and great altitudes of modern hang gliders, some regulations may be instituted. If they are, they will probably be little more than advisory. Provided fliers are careful. According to Cliff Elbl, of the FAA, "I eventually expect to see regulations to the effect that no person may operate an airplane or hang glider in a manner which might endanger himself or others."

To date, the FAA has made the following recommendations regarding hang gliding:

1. PURPOSE. Since the sport of "hang gliding" or "sky sailing" has become popular, numerous questions have arisen as to the FAA position on the regulation and operation of these vehicles. The purpose of this Advisory Circular is to suggest safety parameters for the operation of "hang gliders" and to present the current FAA intent with respect to the regulation and operation of those vehicles.

2. DEFINITION. For purpose of this Advisory Circular, "hang glider" means an unpowered, single place vehicle whose launch and landing capability depends entirely on the legs of the occupant and whose ability to remain in flight is generated by natural air currents only.

3. BACKGROUND. There has been a recent revival of popular interest in the almost forgotten art of powerless flight. This is now being accomplished by very light vehicles that are self-launched and unpowered. The sport is referred to as "hang gliding" or "sky sailing." New materials, modern construction techniques, improved knowledge of stability and control requirements, and imaginative configurations have all been applied. Coupled with low cost and aviation adventure that has attracted both young and old, this increasingly popular sport is expected to grow dramatically in the near future. . . . Several corporations have been formed to manufacture these craft, along with a

manufacturer's association that intends to provide minimum materials criteria to ensure safe construction. Numerous clubs have been formed, and many may be formed in the future, which will provide safety guidance through both operational control and educational media.

4. REGULATORY INFORMATION. The FAA is interested in this activity, but at this time does not have sufficient data and information with respect to "hang glider" design and operational capabilities to make any determination as to the need for new specific action. It is the FAA's intent to observe the growth and safety status of this activity as it progresses and to continually assess the need for FAA involvement. The following, however, are certain regulatory areas of which "hang glider" operators should take cognizance:

a. FEDERAL AVIATION REGULATIONS, PART 101. Part 101 specifies rules applicable to kite operations. Those rules are applicable to any vehicle intended to be flown at the end of a rope, having as its only means of support the force of the wind moving past its surfaces, and that is not capable of sustained flight when released from its tether. No person should operate a "hang glider" at the end of a surface towline without first becoming fully familiar with Part 101.

b. FEDERAL AVIATION REGULATIONS, SECTIONS 91.17 AND 91.18. Section 91.17 provides rules applicable to the towing by an aircraft of gliders as that term is defined in FAR Part 1. Section 91.18 (a) provides, in part, that no pilot of a civil aircraft may tow anything with that aircraft (other than under 91.17) except in accordance with the terms of a certificate of waiver issued by the Administrator.

5. SAFETY SUGGESTIONS. The following guidelines are suggested for the use of all participants in "hang gliding," manufacturers of "hang gliders" and operating clubs.

a. SUGGESTIONS RELATING TO OPERATION OF THE VEHI-
CLE:

(1) Limit altitude to 500 feet above the general terrain. It must be remembered, however, that there are certain aircraft operations conducted below 500 feet above the terrain and "hang glider" operators should be alert to this.

(2) Do not fly them within controlled airspace, specifically a control zone, airport traffic area, or within five miles of the boundary of an uncontrolled airport unless authorized by airport authorities.

(3) Do not fly them within any prohibited or restricted area without prior permission from the controlling or using agency as appropriate.

(4) Do not fly them within 100 feet horizontally of, or at any altitude over, buildings, populated places, or assemblages of persons.

(5) Remain clear of clouds.

(6) Questions regarding operations in conflict with the above recommended safety parameters should be discussed with the nearest FAA district office.

b. SUGGESTIONS TO MANUFACTURERS AND CLUBS:

(1) Develop criteria for materials and construction techniques. (It is recommended that aircraft quality hardware and materials be utilized in construction as appropriate.)

(2) Ensure that adequate quality control procedures are utilized during manufacture of the vehicle.

(3) Pay particular attention to ensure that a good training program is established. (The United States Hang Glider Association can be helpful in this area.) Students should be taught early to recognize their individual limitations as well as the limitations of the "hang glider."

(4) Provide adequate instructions in "do-it-yourself" kits so that proper hardware is utilized and good construction techniques are employed.

(5) Coordinate with local municipalities and property owners for recognized flying sites.

(6) Establish strong safety programs and distribute safety related materials to clubs, associations, and operators of "hang gliders."

(7) Develop close coordination with the Federal Aviation Administration.

(8) Operators of "hang gliders" should be encouraged to wear protective clothing, including a helmet.

6. CONCLUSION. The Federal Aviation Administration is willing to devote time and effort, within reason, to assist manufacturers and clubs during this developmental period. District Offices are encouraged to work with manufacturers and clubs so that the sport is conducted in a safe manner. Safety related materials developed by clubs and manufacturers' associations will be disseminated to all Regions as it [sic] is developed. Appropriate material coming to the attention of field offices should be forwarded to Headquarters as well as related safety information developed by local FAA personnel. The "hang glider" community should, on the other hand, make a vigorous effort to develop safety criteria and instructions usable in the manufacture and operation of "hang gliders."

7. DISTRIBUTION. This Advisory Circular should be given the widest distribution possible by district offices to ensure that all persons interested in this activity are aware of the information contained in this document.

Hang gliding is popular around the world, and not all countries are taking as liberal a view toward the sport as the United States' FAA. Some countries have regulations, and others are considering them. Most of the regulations, however, are more involved with the protection of the nonflying public than with hang gliders themselves.

France, for example, is considering a stringent list of regulations to protect people on the ground and another series of regulations regarding the quality of materials used in French-made hang gliders. In Switzerland hang gliders must be registered like any other aircraft, and a license is needed by a hang glider pilot. There is also a minimum age limit of sixteen years.

In Germany hang gliders are subject to the tough regulations covering all aircraft. In Austria regulations are being set up, and in other countries there are official government regulations covering hang gliding.

The hang glider pilot in the United States is not encumbered by rules and regulations. The FAA suggestions previously listed are clear, concise, and reasonable.

The possibility of being regulated is another reason hang gliding pilots have become so vocal about safety and proper procedures. The more problems that occur within the sport, the more it will become obvious that the sport is unable to regulate itself. Therefore, you owe it to yourself and to the sport to fly safely.

6/SAFETY

Recently a young hang glider was flying Yosemite, which hardly describes what he was really doing. "Flying Yosemite" means running to the edge and taking off from rocky Glacier Point, a sheer cliff of more than 3,000 feet. After a flight of ten to fifteen minutes, the gliders land on a grassy meadow in beautiful Yosemite Valley, California.

Strict rules controlling such flights are carefully enforced by rangers from the park service. In addition, no flights are permitted after eight o'clock in the morning to prevent traffic buildups along valley roads as motorists stop to watch the colorful gliders.

This young pilot, however, forgot one of the primary rules of hang gliding: After *any* change in its assembly, a glider should be test-flown off a low, safe hill to be sure everything is still adjusted correctly. This pilot's glider had been rerigged, torn down, and put back together. He assembled his glider, stepped into his harness, hooked up his sling, and ran off the high edge of Glacier Point. Anyone who has ever been there will recall the sheer drop.

Almost instantly the glider fell off on one wing and began to sideslip. The pilot fought desperately for control, and the glider began to turn, but the turn was making matters worse by carrying the glider directly into the face of the cliff. Only by sheer strength and will did he finally get it turned away from the cliff, and from there he fought his way to the ground for a hard landing.

He had not tested the glider on a low hill. If he had, he would have found the problem in the rerigging that was pulling one wing and causing the glider to turn sharply.

A similar incident occurred with a pilot who was so anxious to fly that he neglected to preflight his glider after setting it up. He didn't notice that he had pinched the fabric· of the sail on one side, where the crossbar is attached to the leading edge. As a result, the billow angle, or amount of air under the wing, was much less on that side of the glider. A preflight inspection would doubtless have disclosed the problem, but as he took off from a several-hundred-foot cliff, the glider immediately turned to the right and began to spiral to the ground. The spiral tightened as the glider dropped. He was caught in an ever-reducing series of 360° turns, a very dangerous situation. For the last fifty or sixty feet he was in an uncontrolled free-fall. Fortunately the landing was in deep sand, so he was only shaken and bruised and not seriously injured.

Sometimes a problem with a glider might not be obvious

or readily discernible. The answer in this situation is to fold up the glider and go home until the problem is solved. One pilot was testing a glider off a 4,400-foot peak from which long soaring flights could be made. Because he noted a tail-heavy condition, he changed his suspension sling to bring it over the front of the control bar, thereby violating an important rule. Then he compounded his problem by not testing the new arrangement on a gentle slope.

His flight was one of fear and struggle as he pushed all the way out on the bar and still only barely maintained the glider's attitude and trim. He was on the very edge of being completely out of control, of falling to his death. He fought and fought, feeling his strength wane, for it is a real effort to battle against an unresponsive glider. Finally, as he reached the ground, he used his last ounce of strength to flare for a landing. The landing was hard on both him and the glider, though he was not killed.

Any hang gliding school will lecture at some length on the care you must take in setting up your glider before any flight. Then, after you have set up, the instructors will tell you to preflight, or check the work you have just completed with such care. Finally they will stress the importance of testing your glider on a low hill after *any* change has been made in its basic structure or rigging.

The trouble is, sometimes even the sheer exhilaration of hang gliding can get you into trouble. This was the case when Rich Grigsby, a mainstay of the United States Hang Gliding Association and editor of *Ground Skimmer* magazine, became involved in a humorous crash in Ventura County, California.

Grigsby, a hang gliding teacher, is a superb pilot. He is a

man who carefully inspects his equipment, reads the wind with skill, and never flies when his own good judgment tells him to stay on the ground.

This particular day the weather was fine, and Grigsby, also involved in glider manufacture, was test-flying. His glider was performing perfectly, and before he realized it, he was far out over the ocean. He looked back at the hazy shoreline and knew he suddenly had a very special problem. He wasn't going to fall, his glider was flying fine, he felt good, and the wind was perfect.

His only problem was, he might *drown*.

Turning gently, he began to fly back toward the shoreline. He could see that it was going to be an extremely close matter, a flip of a coin. He might make it to the smooth sand or he might not.

He called upon every bit of the skill he had developed over the years to stretch his flight to the last possible inch. On-shore they were watching him as he sank lower and lower but glided closer and closer.

Gary Vallé, a friend of Grigsby's, remembers the landing with a smile. "Rich really tried to make it back. Finally he skimmed in, bounced off the top of a breaking wave, and landed with a great splash in the very last foot of water. He wasn't hurt at all, but his glider was completely destroyed. There is nothing worse on a glider than a water landing. Rich was sitting in this foot of water just off the beach with pieces of his glider floating all around."

The cardinal safety rule of hang gliding, as perhaps it should be of almost every other endeavor, is "Always maximize your margin of safety."

Rich Grisby, who flew too far out over the ocean at Ventura County, shoots himself into the air over Pacific Coast Highway.

If you have a chance to hang glide one way or another, choose the safe way. For example, a flying site has a choice of two takeoff spots. Both spots are relatively safe, one being slightly safer than the other. You have a brand-new, fully tested glider with an outstanding sail pattern of blues and reds. You yourself are a good pilot.

Here's the dilemma: One of the takeoff spots, the one slightly less safe, is in full view of a Sunday afternoon crowd of spectators, including several people you would really like to impress. The other spot is out of their immediate view.

From which spot do you take off?

Always maximize your margin of safety.

Take off from the hidden spot.

At many areas you can soar if you stay close enough to the hill. Soaring is one of the outstanding experiences of hang gliding, but flying close to a hill or cliff face is definitely not as safe as flying away from it. So to maximize your margin of safety, fly farther out and soar somewhat less.

Hang gliding is fun, exciting, challenging, and relatively safe, but no matter how you soften it the sport has a real potential for danger. You *can* get hurt—or worse—flying about in the sky beneath a rigid or flexible wing. It happens more and more as the sport gains more and more enthusiasts.

Hang gliding can be compared to motorcycling in regard to safety. The real danger is not with beginners or experts. The pilots who are most likely to get in trouble are the intermediates, those enthusiasts who have lost their fear of the glider and the elements. These are the pilots who are so supremely confident that they will try anything. *Nothing* frightens them.

There are motorcycle riders who, at the beginning, have a

very high respect for their machine. They know how seriously the motorcycle can hurt them if they fail to handle it correctly. Experienced riders are the same. They have ridden for thousands of miles and have regained their respect for their bikes. They have seen riders in the ditch.

It is the middle-experience riders who most often get hurt. Middle-experience hang gliders tend to encounter trouble more often, too.

Conservative fliers enjoy the sport and live to tell about it. But isn't that boring, just soaring around and never trying anything zany?

If it is, get out of hang gliding and into another sport.

You will always find someone making a tight turn into a cliff. Even though the rules say never to turn into a cliff, some pilots do it anyway. They have turned in before, they have plenty of room to make it, and turning into the cliff is far more convenient than turning out and perhaps losing altitude that will have to be fought for later.

But it is the flier who will *not* make such a turn under *any* circumstance who will never get hurt by turning into a cliff.

Wearing a helmet is another conservative precaution. Chances are you are never going to get hurt by banging your head on a rock or on the glider. But if you are wearing a helmet, you are *sure* your head will be safe.

It is not very funny to say, "It wasn't the fall that hurt you, but the sudden stop," to a hang glider pilot who has fallen. The air is not people's natural element. Like the ocean, it can be unforgiving. So you, the glider pilot, must maximize your margin of safety by taking advantage of every possible safety measure.

It is easy to forget sometimes.

During a recent hang gliding altitude record attempt a pilot and his crew thought they had considered *everything*. They had the proper instruments, clothing, and oxygen. The glider was to be carried aloft by a hot-air balloon with the pilot in his sling in position underneath. At the proper altitude the glider pilot would merely pull a release rope and the glider would fall free. It had worked before and it would work again. Safety was a prime consideration in the air and during ground handling and preflight.

The altitude was reached, and the pilot, now on oxygen, looked at his situation. His instruments were correct; his oxygen was flowing; his high-altitude suit was working; he was comfortable and in command. He was ready.

He jerked the release rope attaching the kingpost of his glider to the gondola of the balloon.

Instantly he was hanging in a vertical position. The nose of the glider was still attached to the balloon by a safety rope. The pilot was hanging from the control bar (and his harness, of course). He couldn't reach the release, and the entire record attempt seemed doomed. The balloon would have to land to free the glider.

Finally, however, the rope gave way, the glider fell free, and the pilot recovered trim. The flight was a resounding success, establishing a new record.

But those few moments of hanging by the glider's nose from the bottom of the balloon were hectic and scary. Even the finest pilots and crews can slip up momentarily.

In the Second World War pilots were faced with "gremlins." These were unpleasant, invisible little creatures who went about doing mischievous and dangerous things to airplanes. Gremlins even went along on flights, interfering with instruments, fouling guns, freezing carburetors, and generally making complete nuisances of themselves. Gremlins are back, and hang glider pilots must be aware of them.

Part of the safety problem is that the type of people who are attracted to hang gliding are the same type as those who would fly a fast airplane into combat or go for an altitude record or do something else that the more timid wouldn't consider. They are people who *do* things, who face challenges and live life to the fullest. They are more competitive than most people. They would rather lose than not attempt to win.

But competitiveness sometimes gets out of hand. You feel you are in command and able to try that one last thing everyone says shouldn't be done. Whether it is turning into a cliff with a tight turn and grazing the rocks with your wing tip or trying a series of 360° turns at a low altitude, you know that others have done it and survived, so why not you? You're just as good as they are. So you try it.

Chances are good that you will survive in fine shape with a smooth and pleasant flight, but what if you don't?

Then you are a statistic.

A pilot at Point Fermin, in California, had his attention called to a stripped bolt on his glider. Another flier had noticed it and suggested that the fault be corrected immediately, certainly before another flight.

"One more flight," promised the first pilot, "then I'll quit for the day and replace the bolt."

Why? Who knows? Perhaps for the same reason that we all sometimes drive our cars at over the speed limit, certain in the skill we have and the knowledge that "everything is under control."

The bolt failed on that last flight, the wing folded, and the young pilot was killed in the fall.

In another accident, a teenager was paralyzed from below his neck because he was flying a homemade glider (not recommended) at a brand-new site, without preflight instruction (not recommended), with a new harness (not recommended before testing) in a new position (the same). He misjudged his glide angle and crashed into some bushes along a creek bed. From there he fell the last 25 feet to the dry creek bottom. His helmet (recommended) probably saved his life, but his spine was severely injured. With luck he might recover.

Another pilot was experimenting with low-altitude 360° turns. He was warned by other pilots that he hadn't gained enough experience even to consider such stunts. Still he went back up, entered a three-sixty pattern, and never pulled out. He was killed.

If you can tell yourself you will fly but will never attempt maneuvers which are proved to be dangerous or beyond your ability and still *mean* it six months after you have had the clean wind in your face and have gained perfect control over your glider, then you should probably continue. If not, if you find you are reneging on your promise to yourself, park your glider and take up some other sport before you get hurt.

Manufacturers are trying to help the brave ones (spell that f-o-o-l-i-s-h) by working on equipment such as helmets that help to protect the neck and lightweight flight jackets with built-in air-expandable cushions for severe impacts.

Gerald Albiston, president of Free Flight Systems, made some excellent points regarding safety in an article in *Hang Glider* magazine. He feels that suitable flight gear—helmets, gloves, boots, and other protective clothing—should be stressed more strongly to students just learning the sport. He also urges hang gliding instructors to emphasize the need for slow progression to higher takeoff points.

Beginning pilots, according to his article, should be discouraged from flying in winds above 12 miles per hour and from attempting 360° turns. And all stunt flying—whip stalls, climbing onto the control bar, hanging upside down on the swing seat, and any other stunts of this type—should be absolutely forbidden.

Sometimes young pilots must be protected from themselves.

7/ RECORDS AND
COMPETITION

Perhaps it is an admirable quality, perhaps it is a flaw in character, but American sportsmen in almost any endeavor have an ingrained streak of competitiveness. It begins when we are young. Remember? The boy next door walked the fence halfway, so you had to walk it *all* the way. The girl down the street climbed to the first branch of the tree, so you had to go to the second branch.

Good or bad, that's the way it is with us, and hang glider pilots are no exception. In fact, considering the high-risk element, they might be considered even more competitive than most.

An example is Rudy Kishazy, a Plymouth, Michigan, electrician who decided to set an altitude record by jumping off the highest point in Europe, Mont Blanc, France. There were many safety preparations, including a glider specially built by Bill Bennett for the occasion.

However, while skiing down the sharply sloping side of the very top of a 15,766-foot mountain peak in 15-below-zero cold, with the dropoff approaching just ahead, Kishazy suddenly realized the air might be too thin to support glider flight.

He also realized it was far too late to stop.

Here's what happened, in Kishazy's own words:

The breathing is difficult and it sounds strange . . . it is very loud. I began to get tired and sluggish and a little headachy. Finally the helicopter reappeared with the cameramen on board. It was 4:00 P.M. when I got the signal to go ahead. I squeezed the [control] bar. I wasn't afraid but I did feel like fighting. I was getting very mad and I felt I just had to win. As I took off I couldn't see too well. I skied down the northeast side which is a 45–50° ice wall. I was just speeding and speeding. I heard a sharp noise when the sail was grabbed by the wind, warning me that I had reached take-off speed. I pushed the bar, but no response. My thoughts began getting mixed up.

At that point Kishazy was speeding down the sharp ice-covered slope with a 15,000-foot dropoff dead ahead, and his glider was not working.

Suddenly a funny feeling jerked me awake, as if a fast elevator had stopped. The wind was blowing in my face and I was shouting "I made it . . . I made it!"

The view was breathtaking and I was just speeding, fighting with the turbulences. Catching a strong updraft, I just glided. I lost the mountain, I just shot out of space. It looked like the whole world stopped and I felt as if I didn't belong to it any-

Rudy Kishazy during his world record altitude flight off Mont Blanc in France in 1973.

more. The clouds were dense and getting into my way, then slowly I could see through the clouds and fog into the valley.

Finally Kishazy landed, but for another long moment he held the control bar, trying to extend his dream as long as possible. He realized he was tired, very tired. Then a man walked to him and offered him a glass of wine, and he knew he had set a world altitude record.

Though the Kishazy record no longer stands as the highest man has ever flown in a hang glider, it is still the highest hang gliding flight ever made from solid ground. A new record was set by Dennis Burton when he was dropped from a balloon at an altitude of 22,500 feet at Rosamond, near Edwards Air Force Base in the desert country of southern California.

Burton, a twenty-three-year-old hang gliding pilot from California, began as a backup pilot for Free Flight Systems, but when the scheduled pilot dropped out after several months of preparation, Burton stepped in. He had been trained in equipment use, parachute jumping, oxygen techniques, and all the other necessary skills for such a dangerous flight, and he had developed a harness that would allow him to break away from his glider quickly in case of trouble.

At five-thirty in the dark of the early morning, the balloon was inflated, but almost immediately the wind began to blow, and the balloon was deflated as a safety precaution. Conditions improved, the balloon was inflated again, and again the wind velocity increased . . . but it was too late. The balloon glider combination was off the ground, and the 30-mile-per-hour winds could no longer stop the great adventure.

All was serene in the air, and in an hour and three minutes

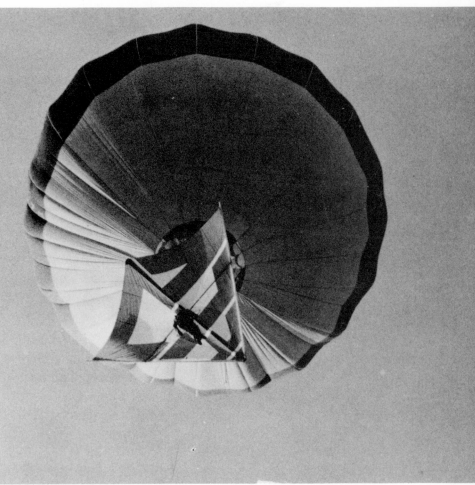

A straight up view of Dennis Burton's glider being lifted by the balloon before Burton's record drop.

the glider was at the drop altitude of 22,500 feet. Burton was freezing in the 70-below-zero cold in spite of his high-altitude clothing (it was more than half an hour after he landed that the feeling returned to his hands), but otherwise he was ready. The signal came. The unit was being monitored by the FAA at its nearest control facility at Palmdale, so Burton ordered a descent of the balloon.

A balloon dropping a hang glider must be descending at the time of release, for two reasons: The sail of the glider must be filled before the moment of drop, and the balloon pilot must be aware that he is dropping a several-hundred-pound ballast and will quickly begin to rise.

Burton tripped the release and fell away. Below, much of the southern California desert region was spread out. He looked back up at the balloon to orient himself, but already it was far above him. He was gliding downward, and at the same time the balloon had shot up to 26,000 feet at his release.

For forty-five peaceful minutes Burton followed roads far down on the ground. As one road would wind up into the desert foothills and stop at an old abandoned mine or ghost village, he would pick another and begin to follow it. His hands were numb from the cold, but otherwise he was in control and enjoying the flight. With a strong tailwind he could not expect his ground crew to keep up with him, so he continued to follow desert roads.

Gradually he came down. Finally spotting a home in the desert, with a very convenient wind sock along an old runway, he picked his landing spot. As he swept in, stalled, and gently touched down, the people in the house stared in amazement.

The nearest high point was miles away. Where had he come from?

Grinning, Dennis Burton explained that he had just set a new hang gliding altitude record, and when they told him where he was, an abandoned movie lot at El Mirage, he realized he had set a distance record of 24 miles as well. Pilot Rich Grigsby tied Burton's distance record with an amazing flight from Sylmar to Palmdale in California. This 24-mile flight was recognized by the USHGA.

There are many unusual records in the young sport of hang gliding and constant attempts at new ones. Chuck Slusarcsyk flew from Edgewater Park, Cleveland, Ohio, and landed at Erieau, Ontario, Canada. The flight took 1 hour 45 minutes and set two world records. It was the first time anybody took off in one country and landed in another.

The standing endurance record was set in Hawaii by Dave Vincent, who enjoyed an amazing hang gliding flight of 13 hours 5 minutes.

These records and others will surely be broken, and there are a large number of hang glider pilots who answer this with a loud "So what!" These fliers feel that endurance flights and altitude records only prove that the wind blows longer or higher on certain days and that once a pilot has soared for an hour or so he has proved his ability to fly.

Distance is another mark some hang gliders reach for. Mark Clarkson flew for more than 17 miles across the desert near Phoenix, Arizona. Some hang glider pilots have reached the same altitudes sailplanes reach, and the gliders are carried great distances by the winds.

The majority of competitive-minded hang glider pilots are

turning to the sponsored and sanctioned contests becoming more and more available around the United States and around the world. The major meets are most often sponsored by an interested manufacturing firm, not necessarily of hang gliders, and sanctioned by the major hang gliding association, the United States Hang Gliding Association. This is a rapidly growing organization of several thousand members that began in Southern California and soon attracted members from across the country. In 1973 the members voted to change the name from Southern California Hang Glider Association to the present USHGA.

The association's bylaws state its primary purpose: ". . . to engage in the development, study, and use of fuel-less flight systems and aircraft capable of being launched by human power alone, to make knowledge relating to these subjects available, and to organize meets where the testing and flying of such systems and aircraft will be encouraged."

The USHGA has an informative and entertaining monthly magazine called *Ground Skimmer,* which keeps members informed on latest techniques and equipment.

Also a part of the USHGA is an accident review board made up of skilled pilots. These board members examine each reported accident to determine its true cause and ways to avoid such accidents in the future. Each month in *Ground Skimmer* a review of the investigated accidents is presented to members.

Liability insurance is available to USHGA members at a reasonable rate.

Perhaps one of the most important of all the activities of the USHGA is the "hang rating" program. Because hang gliding is as yet unregulated by government bodies, just about anyone can fly just about anywhere. Fliers must get permission from private land owners, but otherwise the sport is free.

Under such conditions accidents are certain to result. Fliers train on a bunny hill one weekend and the next weekend attempt to take off from an advanced location. Because most make it, the habit continues. But a few do not make it for the simple reason that they are not yet skilled enough to handle the higher altitudes, the trickier wind and weather conditions, and the more advanced flying techniques.

The hang rating program of the USHGA is an effort to control the sport from within, to prevent accidents before such accidents call the attention of the regulating bodies to the sport. Throughout the country expert fliers are chosen to become observers, examiners, and instructors. These pilots are assigned areas near their homes, and they become responsible for issuing cards with hang ratings for hang glider pilots who request this service. The ratings advance from one to five as the pilot's skill increases. Five is extremely difficult to get, demanding not only superb skill as a hang glider pilot but also perfect attitude toward the sport. Cards are issued to pilots who have passed the requirements for each rating. The Hang One rating is issued to pilots who have passed the basic requirements. A pilot who wishes to fly off Glacier Point at Yosemite National Park must have a Hang Four rating with a "Cliff Launch" addendum.

It is the plan of the USHGA to hang rate each prominent hang gliding site in the country according to its difficulty and firmly to suggest that only pilots with cards equal to or over that rating be permitted to fly there. An easy area might have only a Hang One or Hang Two rating, whereas a very difficult, advanced flight area would probably be a Hang Four.

Write to the USHGA (see Appendix) for more information on its hang rating program and membership in the organization. A beginning hang glider pilot can greatly benefit from associating himself with experts who will guide him as he learns.

The USHGA sanctions and publicizes many meets throughout the country each month. At a typical hang gliding meet several hundred pilots show up with a wide variety of gliders, both flexible and fixed-wing types. If the meet is a major one, there will probably be displays by manufacturers in the landing area as well as refreshment stands, rest rooms, and other conveniences.

The pilots are invited to compete in either an invitational meet, in which the entry list is closed, or an open meet, in which pilots must qualify to compete. The idea of qualification is to weed out the inexperienced pilots as well as those just having a bad day.

Qualification at a hang gliding meet consists of completing a series of tasks. One task is an "aerial slalom." The pilot must take off, fly through the "gate" between the pylons or points placed on the ground, then turn back around each one in a gradual figure eight. After this maneuver he must go to a distant point and back to the target in the landing area. If he goes too far, he won't make it back, but if he doesn't go far enough, he is penalized by the judges. He is awarded ten points for each correct maneuver and then an extra number of points if he can land directly on the target in the landing area.

Another task is to turn around pylons in a lazy S, then hit a target on the ground in the landing area. Still another task is a speed run, in which the pilot must go around the pylons and hit the target, the fastest one getting the most points.

Each of these tasks requires solid judgment and real skill in handling the hang glider.

On the ground, judges selected for their own knowledge and skill watch each flier carefully and award the points. Most of the judges are hang glider pilots themselves and understand the difficulty of the tasks.

The pilots with the most points compete in the finals. Finals are generally exhibitions of exactly the same skills; only the courses are made more intricate, with greater demands on the pilots.

Many pilots have suggested that all hang gliding meets be broken down into classes, and some are now being conducted in this way. Gliders might be rated according to their wing-loading type: Rogallo, Seagull, monoplane, and flying wings. Pilots might be rated according to their flying time and previous meets. Some meets today have pilots rated as A competitors and B competitors, depending on their experience and ability. But rated or unrated, to win a hang gliding meet is indeed an accomplishment.

8/WHERE DO WE GO FROM HERE?

Hang gliding is here to stay. The sport has changed from one of a few daredevil fliers under plastic and bamboo to an activity as safe as the pilot wants to make it, with equipment that continues to advance in safety and sophistication.

The flood of modern accessories to the sport and continuing research on glider shape indicates that everything is still moving. Even Gary Vallé feels the ultimate glider is still in the future.

"Rogallos will still be recognizable as Rogallos, but the configuration will change," he says. As subtle changes are made in the shape, performance will improve.

As time passes, the sport will become better organized. Meets will be more regulated. According to some, the Federal Aviation Administration will sooner or later be forced to take a hard look at this activity that allows a pilot to remain in the air for long periods and over extended distances. Hang gliding will lose its image of that of a handful of thrill seekers and become as accepted as soaring, motorcycling, and scuba diving. The USHGA maintains an increasing membership application rate, indicating that the rapid growth is continuing.

As the sport expands, accessories grow in importance. Some are for safety and improved flying; others are for beauty and comfort.

VARIOMETERS. It is very difficult to discern subtle changes in altitude, even from heights of a few dozen feet. Yet a knowledge of precise altitude is very important to a hang glider pilot. He might be attempting to "core" a thermal (stay completely inside the rising column of air) or soar a ridge or cliff line, both of which require a precise judgment of altitude changes.

The variometer is an accessory which solves the altitude problem. This device is carried up with the pilot and gives an accurate indication of whether the glider is gaining or losing altitude. It may read by a change in sound or by a dial-type indicator. In either case, it tells the pilot by using barometric pressure whether he is going up or down.

AIR-SPEED INDICATORS. These dials and devices may be used on the glider itself or at the takeoff and landing sites. On the glider, indicators range from simple ribbons tied to the flying wires to more complicated hand-held and glider-mounted instruments that give the pilot an indication of the air speed. On the ground, indicators may be wind socks or ribbons tied to a pole. From the simplest to the most complicated, indicators all work by the force of air moving across or through them.

Glider pilot Jack Franklin shows one type of altitude finder, a wrist-mounted dial indicator.

SAILFEATHERS.   These are somewhat controversial accessories. Some manufacturers believe in them and others do not.

The argument revolving around them is mainly scientific and has to do with the forces of lift and drag, the center of gravity, and other flight factors. Basically, the point of the discussion is that a hang glider pilot in a vertical dive has a real problem. The wind is passing across both sides of the sail, top and bottom, with equal speed, creating what is known as a "flag dive." The flapping sail has no lift and thus gives the pilot no control to pull out of the dive. At the moment it is not just a matter of shoving forward on the control bar. Since the pilot and his glider are free-falling, new physical laws come into play.

Some manufacturers have produced the sailfeather as a method of recovery from a vertical dive. In a flag dive the

Here Jack Franklin mounts a sailfeather on his glider as a part of his set up routine.

sailfeather, attached to the rear of the glider, is in a position to create a certain small amount of lift of its own. This lift moves the tail of the glider around the center of gravity of the glider and pilot, thus placing the nose slightly back into the passing wind. If all other factors are equal, the sail fills immediately and control is restored.

According to the manufacturers who include this small extra sail on their gliders, it has no real measurable effect on normal flight. The best idea, of course, is never to dive that steeply in the first place, but the addition of an inexpensive sailfeather does seem to be a good insurance policy just in case.

In fairness to manufacturers who do not use the sailfeather, it should be pointed out that some of them feel the Rogallo shape has a natural tendency to pull out of a steep dive if simply left alone, and others believe a quick push on the control bar, in spite of any laws of physics, will jerk the nose into the wind much more quickly and easily than a sailfeather. The use of a sailfeather does not come into consideration until a pilot has advanced to altitudes where a long dive is possible. When you reach that point, you will have talked to some pilots who use this extra wing and others who do not, and you will be able to make your own decision. More information on sailfeathers can be obtained from Sunbird Gliders (see Appendix) .

DEFLEXERS.   These are also somewhat controversial. Deflexers consist of a series of wires and braces that, when added to a glider, tend to improve the sail's aerodynamic efficiency by reducing the wing spar deflection, or bend. This is accomplished by "bracing" the leading edges—triangulating each spar with an adjustable cable and a "deflexer blade." Also known as wing posts, outriggers, wing wires, or leading edge cables, deflexers are now used by many top fliers on their gliders.

Whether or not you should use deflexers is a personal choice. If you are still carrying your glider up and down smaller hills, you probably should not use them. The extra wires will only complicate assembly and ground handling. But if you are involved in long flights or competition flying, they should certainly be considered. More information on deflexers can be obtained from Ultralight Products (see Appendix).

ROBOT PILOTS.   Robots are being designed to fly gliders in the place of test pilots. One company has two such mechanical men in the design phase, one hydraulic and the other air-actuated. The robots operate on servos—radio-controlled mechanisms—and can imitate either a seated or a prone pilot. With the use of robots, manufacturers can design, construct, and fly completely new and different gliders without risking human injury. Complete test-flight programs are planned for the robots, including dive recovery, stall recovery, and other flight problems.

GLOVES.   Several companies market gloves similar to those worn by motocross motorcycle riders to protect the hand of the hang glider pilot when landing. There are also knee and elbow pads available for the same purpose.

HELMETS.   A few pilots complain about helmets, but most realize that from the first flight off a bunny hill to competition flying, wearing a helmet is a wise decision. In fact, almost all of today's competitions require that the pilots wear helmets.

A *deflexer blade and cables on the leading spar of the "Casper the Ghost" glider of George Barker.*

Hang gliding helmets are lightweight and have open or uncovered earholes so the pilot can hear the wind in the sail. They are relatively inexpensive and are highly recommended for that rare occasion when a landing is not quite as polished as it might be.

BACKPACK MOTOR.   The thought of motorizing the pure and unpolluting sport of hang gliding is unpleasant to some hang glider pilots. But others feel the only problem with the sport is the law of "what goes up must come down" applies too strongly. If there was a way to stay up without depending on the vagaries of the wind, it would be a great improvement.

The backpack motor does provide this. It is a 22-pound, 18-horsepower go-kart motor that is mounted with straps and a propeller (with a wire cage guard) to push a hang glider pilot along at up to 25 miles per hour. With the half-gallon fuel tank full, the range is about 60 miles.

Should the need arise, a quick release on the harness provides the pilot with a way to jettison the whole package. A thumb switch on the control bar is available for quick shutoff of the engine.

More information on the backpack motor can be obtained from Bill Bennett's Delta Wing Kites (see Appendix).

Speaking of backpacks, one hang gliding enthusiast who also enjoys rock climbing would like to combine the two sports. He is awaiting the day when a foldable, portable, lightweight glider is built, one that can be backpacked conveniently. He would like to climb to a takeoff point, assemble the glider, and fly as far as possible, then climb again. His dream is to climb and fly all the way across the Rocky Mountains.

Bill Bennett demonstrates the backpack motor for hang gliders.

Why not! Hang gliding is a burgeoning sport. As it grows, it improves in safety, reliability, and available accessory equipment. It is clean and free and leaves no waste.

Why not, indeed.

In the publications listed in the appendix that follows, a wide variety of carrying bags, cartop mounting and carrying brackets, and other hang gliding accessories can be found. Information on any specific glider can be obtained from the manufacturers listed.

APPENDIX

HANG GLIDING PUBLICATIONS

Aviation Book Co.
555 W. Glenoaks Blvd.
Glendale, Calif. 91202

Basic Guide to Rogallo Flight
Flight Realities
1945 Adams Ave.
San Diego, Calif. 92116

Delta Kite Flyer News
Box 483
Van Nuys, Calif. 91408

*Delta, The Hang Gliding
  Handbook*
Haessner Publishing, Inc.
Newfoundland, N.J. 07435

Ground Skimmer Magazine
PO Box 66306
Los Angeles, Calif. 90066

Hang Gliding
Daniel F. Poynter
PO Box 4232–18
Santa Barbara, Calif. 93103

Hang Flight
Eco-Nautics
PO Box 1154
Redlands, Calif. 92373

True Flight
1719 Hillsdale Ave.
San Jose, Calif. 95124

Wings Unlimited
103B W. 37th St.
Topeka, Kans. 66611

HANG GLIDER MANUFACTURERS

Apollo
722 Barrington Road
Streamwood, Ill. 60103

Bonn Industries
434 West Rawson Ave.
Oak Creek, Wis. 53154

Chandelle Corp.
15955 West 5th Ave.
Golden, Colo. 80401

Chuck's Glider Supply
4200 Royalton Road
Brecksville, Ohio 44141

Cloudmen Glidercraft Co.
905 Church St.
Nashville, Tenn. 37203

Condor
The Bird People
Box 943
Sun Valley, Calif. 91352

Delta Wing Kites and
    Gliders, Inc.
PO Box 483
Van Nuys, Calif. 91408

DSK Aircraft Corp.
12676 Pierce St.
Pacoima, Calif. 91331

Dyna-soar, Inc.
3518 Cahuenga Blvd. W.
Hollywood, Calif. 90068

Eipper-formance, Inc.
1840 Oak Street
Torrance, Calif. 90501

Electra Flyer
3110 San Mateo N. E.
Albuquerque, N.M. 87110

Foot-Launched Flyers
1411 Hyne
Brighton, Mich. 48116

Free Flight Systems, Inc.
12424 Gladstone Ave.
Sylmar, Calif. 91342

Hawk Industries
5111 Santa Fe St.
San Diego, Calif. 92109

Icarus
PO Box 59
Cupertino, Calif. 95104

J. L. Enterprises
1150 Old Country Rd.
Belmont, Calif. 94022

Kitty Hawk Hang Gliders
3202 San Mateo N. E.
Albuquerque, N.M. 87110

Kitty Hawk Kites
Route 158 Bypass
 (at Jockey Ridge)
Nags Head, N.C. 27959

Kondor Kite Co.
PO Box 603
Lewisville, Texas 75067

Man Flight Systems
PO Box 375
Marlboro, Mass. 01752

Manta Products
1647 E. 14th Street
Oakland, Calif. 94606

Muller Kites Ltd.
PO Box 4063, Postal Station C
Calgary, Alberta T2T5M9
Canada

Omega Hang Gliders
Box 1671
Santa Monica, Calif. 90406

Pacific Gull
1321 Calle Valle (Unit F)
San Clemente, Calif. 92672

Phantom Wing, Inc.
PO Box 6044
Concord, Calif. 94524

Pliable Moose Delta Wing,
 Inc.
1382 Caddy Lane
Wichita, Kans. 67212

Sailbird Flying Machines
3123A N. El Paso
Colorado Springs, Colo. 80907

Seagull Aircraft, Inc.
1554 5th Street
Santa Monica, Calif. 90401

Skycraft, Inc.
615 Ruberta Ave.
Glendale, Calif. 91201

Sky Sport, Inc.
Box 441
Whitman, Mass. 02382

Solo Flight
930 W. Hoover Ave.
Orange, Calif. 92667

Sport Wings, Inc.
22 N. 2nd Street
Lafayette, Ind. 47902

True Flight
1719 Hillsdale Ave.
San Jose, Calif. 95124

Sport Kites, Inc.
1202C E. Walnut
Santa Ana, Calif. 92704

UP, Inc. (Ultralite Products)
137 Oregon St.
El Segundo, Calif. 90245

Sunbird Gliders
21420 Chase St. #7
Canoga Park, Calif. 91304

Velderrain Hang Gliders
PO Box 314
Lomita, Calif. 90717

Sun Sail Corp.
6753 E. 47th Avenue Dr.
Denver, Colo. 80216

Westerly Sails
3511 Midway Dr.
San Diego, Calif. 92110

Sun Valley Kite School
17360 Beach Drive, N. E.
Seattle, Wash. 98155

Whitney's Porta-Wing
PO Box 90762
Los Angeles, Calif. 90009

The Nest Airplane Works
1445½ W. 11th Ave.
Eugene, Ore. 97402

Zephyr Aircraft Corp.
25 Mill St.
Glastonbury, Conn. 06066

HANG GLIDING NATIONAL ORGANIZATIONS

United States Hang Gliding
  Association
PO Box 66306
Los Angeles, Calif. 90066

Hang Glider Manufacturers
  Association
137 Oregon St.
El Segundo, Calif. 90245

INDEX

117

THE AUTHOR

Ross R. Olney has written several books for Putnam's, including *Kings of the Drag Strip, Great Dragging Wagons, Kings of Motor Speed, Superstars of Auto Racing,* and, in collaboration with Ron Grable, *The Racing Bugs.* Mr. Olney is an accomplished sailor, skin diver, and photographer. He lives in Ventura, California, with his wife and children.